ROSES AMONG
THE THORNS

ROSES AMONG THE THORNS

Julieanne Gentz

When I was 5 years old, my mother always told me that happiness was the key to life. When I went to school, they asked me what I wanted to be when I grew up. I wrote down, "happy!" They told me I didn't understand the assignment. I told them they didn't understand life.

—John Lennon

Copyright © 2021 by Julieanne Gentz
Print ISBN: 978-1-945116-37-7

Formatting by BB eBooks

All Rights Are Reserved. No part of this book may be used or reproduced in any manner whatsoever without written permission, except in the case of brief quotations embodied in critical articles and reviews.

For My Children

Thank you for being the light in the darkness that has helped me weather so many storms of life.

And for the me that I am today

Throughout all of life's struggles the best advice I have given myself is embodied in a quote by Sangeeta Rana: "Take care of your inner self. Your soul lives there."

Table of Contents

September   1

Forbidden Fruit   3

From Child to Adolescent   5

Rite of Passage   7

October   11

Remembrance   13

Unspoken Thoughts   15

December   17

Introspection   19

Random Observations   21

One or the Other   23

Sometimes   25

Life Descriptions	27
Misconceptions	29
Paradoxes	31
Lament	33
Believe	35
Unicorns and Rainbows	37
Life in the Balance	39
Conquest	41
January	**43**
Alone	45
Muses	47
Memoirs	49
February	**51**
Missing Parts—Changing Hearts	53
Syntax Says It All	55
Time Marches On	57
Imperspicuity	59
Walking Towards the Light	61
The Walk	63

Valley Gardens	65
First Love	67
March	69
Dragons	71
What You Break You Pay For	73
April	75
String Around My Finger	77
About this Book	79
About the Author	81

September

Decisions have never come easy for me. This one is by far the hardest though. What do you use as criteria when you are faced with ending a marriage? Confusion and fear become your constant companions.

Forbidden Fruit

If choices were like apples
waiting to be picked by me,
I'd choose the best so carefully
and leave some on the tree

If decision were the tiny seeds
deep down within the core,
I'd pluck each out with patience,
and try to not keep score.

If life were like the deep red peel
wrapped round about the rest,
I'd take it off quite gingerly,
so as not to fail the test.

And if a storm would come my way
and to the ground I'd fall,
I'd know that it was all God's plan,
and wouldn't mind at all.

For as the days and years passed by
and the fruit faded away,
I'd know the seeds would sprout again
into a tree one day.

So let me live as simply
as an apple on a tree,
with hope, and love, and giving;
please set my spirit free.

From Child to Adolescent

From child to adolescent; girl to woman; wife and mother. Life is a never-ending cycle of changes. Some we make with others, but most we make alone. As I leave my marriage of nearly 20 years and more to foreign surroundings, I take with me remnants of the past, and many questions about the future. And I am alone.

Rite of Passage

As I stand alone watching

my life passes by.

I feel like a stranger

without knowing why.

Who is this person

I thought I once knew?

How did I get here?

What should I do?

Life is a mystery

I don't understand.

I give it my heart

but it won't take my hand.

I know I can make it

In the world on my own.

It's just that I get scared

to do it alone.

I've cried and I've worried,

I'm still scared to death,

but it's time to go on now:

to take a deep breath.

Life is a mystery

I can't comprehend,

but one day its journey

will come to an end.

So, I need to keep living

and doing my best.

Trust in myself and

let God do the rest.

For I've many treasures

yet to uncover.

Hills to climb over

and loves to discover.

Things won't be simple –

might even be tough –

but I believe in myself,

and I pray that's enough.

October

The days come and go, and I wonder. I wonder where we went wrong: what happened to the love we once shared? There are days when I think I will surely die of a broken heart. I feel alone and emotionally abandoned.

Remembrance

Tell me of a time when hope
was not a sunken treasure.
Tell me of a time when love
was given without measure.

Speak of how a caring hug
was given without thinking.
Speak to me of gentle thoughts
as natural as blinking.

Don't tell me of heartaches,
of troubles and of sorrows.
Send to me some sunshine
to brighten my tomorrows.

My hopes are oh so shattered,
and my heart, I fear, is broken.
Tell me of a time when love
was given, not just spoken.

Take me on the wings of hope
and fly me far away.
Tell me that I'll make it –
that all will be ok.

Tell me, oh please tell me,
or I shall fade and die.
Make me smile and make me laugh,
I want no more to cry.

Unspoken Thoughts

I asked for you to love me
in a way you don't know how.
That's why my heart is broken
and my world's in shambles now.

I have a need inside me
that grows stronger with each day.
I'd hoped if I ignored it
that it might go away.

But each day it grows stronger
and is more and more a part
of all of me: My mind, my soul,
my thinking, and my heart.

I want so much to fill this empty
place I feel inside.
But the things I need are phantoms—
they seem to run and hide.

And though I want to stop the hurt
and ache that fills my soul,
I know that it's a healing time,
so one day I'll feel whole.

But now my tears still fall like rain,
thought I would bid them cease.
I pray for the strength to carry on:
For hope, and love, and peace.

December

Fall turns into winter. Days turn into months. I write as an escape valve for the myriad of emotions that churn constantly inside me. I am amazed at the feelings that erupt unannounced into words.

Introspection

I often have thoughts deep inside me
that sometimes cry out to be said.
Some need only be written,
but others are meant to be read.

I don't understand all these stirrings
that come from deep down in my soul.
Are they some type of healing
in my constant search to feel whole?

They pour from my head like a river
and flow from my mind to my pen.
Sometimes I just get them written
and they start all over again.

The words are always in verse form.
The rhymes seem never to cease.
They give to my soul and my spirit
a comforting kind of release.

JULIEANNE GENTZ

If I could but live as my poems do,
so strong, so easy and free.
For you see, in the words that they carry
is the person that really is me.

Random Observations

In trying to salvage the fabric of my life, I have managed to unravel the threads of all those interwoven into its pattern.

I listened with my heart and ignored my head. Now I am paying the price with my spirit.

I don't know what hurts more rights now: The fact that we have no love left between us, or the fact that I can't remember what it is that I should be missing.

I imagine that all inside of me must be full of bruises. Why must you continue the punches?

Why do I fight, if in winning I have lost?
Where do I draw the line on the cost?

One or the Other

Together alone.
Alone together.
Together again?
No.
Never.
Ever.

Sometimes

Sometimes, no matter how hard you look, there are no answers to your questions, only more questions.

Life Descriptions

C N U I N
O F S O
Inside Out
sdrawkcaB
UPSIDE DOWN

All of these are me now.

Misconceptions

I always thought love was forever – a magic that never would die.

I trusted my heart to guide me – but ended up living a lie.

I wanted so bad to love and be loved that I wasn't too careful who I chose to share my life with. Did the same thing happen to you?

I really thought that I loved you, but the meaning never was clear.

I supposed that's why after half a lifetime our lives have ended up here.

I don't think I ever knew you – nor you really knew I:

A realization that's very distressing and makes me ask myself, "WHY?"

And now in retaliation for a love that's faded away,

You continue to torture the memories, day after day after day.

I cry, but that doesn't help me. I yell and scream and get mad.

Sometimes I wish you'd just disappear: You make me feel that bad.

One day I'll love somebody, and all this will be in the past.

I just wish to God, you would leave me alone and let this be over at last.

Paradoxes

Have you ever been so sad that you wanted to cry – but couldn't?

Have you ever wanted tears to come – and tried but they just wouldn't?

Has your heart been oh so broken that you feared that you would die?

Have you ever been too sad that you tried – but couldn't cry?

Have you stood and watched someone you love turn and walk away?

Have you felt the weight of all the world had come on you to stay?

Have you ever fought so hard to win – and when you'd won, you'd lost?

Has your life felt like it's just been hit by a deadly, killing frost?

Have you ever thought of giving up the things you feel are right?

Have you ever thought if all the hurt was really worth the fight?

At one time I've felt all these things – I'm so confused and sad.

Why is it when I stand my ground – it seems to turn out bad?

Lament

Child of mine
with strings on my heart –
what is this nightmare
that's torn us apart?

Child of my own,
created from dreams,
how can it be
life is not what it seems?

Hurt by the sadness
and sorrows of life.
Beaten with conflict.
Tortured with strife.

How can I tell you,
help you to see
that things are not always
what they seem to be?

Child of mine,
the healer is Time.
May its touch bring a solace
to your life and mine.

Believe

I need a little laughter
that I can tuck away
deep down in my pocket
for a sad and lonely day.

I need a little hope
that I can hold inside:
Some self-esteem and confidence
that I don't have to hide.

I need to hold my head up high
and stand my ground at last,
for life is made of fleeting days
that tumble by too fast.

I need to laugh and smile and love
a little more each day—
go searching for the sunshine
that I want to come my way.

Take the laughter from my pocket,
and wear it on my sleeve:
Laugh and smile and hope and love –
but most of all *believe*.

Unicorns and Rainbows

I'm searching for a feeling
that somehow has been lost.
I'm looking for the bridges
that have once before been crossed.

I'm looking for the rainbow
that once I thought I had.
I want to place below it
all that makes me feel so bad.

I long to find a hand to hold,
a caring heart to say
that all this will soon pass away
and bring a brighter day.

But sometimes I feel all alone –
so by myself and sad.
I wonder what those rainbows were
that I once thought I had.

Were they only an illusion
that was soon to disappear?
Where they something I imagined?
Were they never really here?

No, I believe in magic;
in unicorns and dreams.
And I believe that life is not
as lonely as it seems.

I still believe my rainbow
is hooked onto a star.
That someday I will reach it,
though I may travel far.

I'll hop upon a smile
and ride there on moonbeams –
all the while collecting
my pockets full of dreams.

Life in the Balance

The battle was waged and won behind closed doors while I sat outside and waited. I "won", yet we all lost.

Conquest

What does it mean to win?
How do you define victory?
Is it words on paper
that require actions
that don't get taken?

Winning
is in name only
when to win
means
to hurt those you love.

Sometimes
WINNING
means
losing.

January

A new year, with old feelings of loneliness. As the nights grow long and cold, so does my heart. Loneliness is like a bitter cold that I cannot dress properly to ward off.

Alone

I
eat alone,
go places,
sleep,
cry.

A
LONE.

I guess it's really
much different
than
before we parted.
Even
when we were
together
I
was still always
emotionally
A
LONE

Muses

A hand to hold when I'm lonely.
A hug or two when I'm blue.
A smile when the day's been a downer –
that's what I'd like from you.

Some words that show I am special.
A glance that shows me you care.
A gentle hand on my shoulder.
A playful muss of my hair.

Gifts that come from the inside –
not ones that will fade or grow old.
These are the treasures I search for –
that cannot be bought or sold.

I know one day I will find them
and longed for dreams will come true.
Maybe the "X" on the treasure map
will lead me directly to you.

Time drags on . . . and on . . .

Every day brings new heartaches: Their price tags are old memories. I feel confused, beaten, bruised, and very tired.

Memoirs

Places that we used to go –
old friends that we used to know…
Old memories

Broken memories and shattered dreams –
hopes that have pulled apart at the seams…
Old memories

Love that should have lasted forever –
feelings we'll feel together – never…
Old memories

Pick up the pieces and make a new start –
wrap up the fragments that once were my heart…
New Hopes!

February

Valentine's Day. Lovers. Memories. Tears. Heartaches and sadness from bygone years.

Missing Parts—Changing Hearts

LOVER
LOVE
OVER

What a difference
leaving out one
important part makes:
In a word
or
in a relationship

Syntax Says It All

Heart and soul

Heart throb

Heartbeat

Home is where the heart is

Peg 'o my heart

Heartfelt

Heartache

Heartbroken

The words take on

new meaning

when you

experience

them

yourself.

Time Marches On

Time Marches On – Or Perhaps it only crawls, wounded, towards the door.

Though there is never enough time, I always have too much. Though days move by, it is never fast enough. Time stands still while life marches on. My life is on hold – and I'm not sure just what for.

Imperspicuity

TIME,
The weaver of dreams.
The painter of memories.

TIME,
The curse of the old.
The teaser of the young.

TIME,
The prolonger of pain.
The healer of wounds.

TIME,
So many things
to so many people.
Be my friend and walk with me.
Make change a little more bearable.

Walking Towards the Light

Walking towards the light . . . hoping.

There are days when the light at the end of the tunnel shines brighter than others, and I feel strength grow inside me. I have grown to know myself quite well in the past months. I have spent time becoming reacquainted with me and find that hidden away deep inside is a very special person.

I feel like a survivor.
That is because, I am.

The Walk

The woods were dark and dreary as I laid me down to sleep. My legs were sore and aching, and I felt like I could weep. The journey had been arduous – long and hard and slow. I felt the need for shelter, but I had nowhere to go. I looked around about me, but the trees were dark and bare. I felt their eyes upon me: Their haunting steady stare. I looked for leaves to cushion me, a pillow for my head. But rocks and sticks and thorns and burrs made up my simple bed. I closed my eyes and raised my mind to travels I must make. I mapped out routes and byways for the pilgrimage I would take. Yet all that night the sticks and thorns and burrs on which I lay, reminded me that dawn would break and bring a better day. The woods I'd leave behind me. My secret they would keep, how a sad and weary traveller paused there once to sleep: Spent the night on brambles but rose to greet the day. Picked up the pieces of her life; smiled and walked away.

Valley Gardens

From the valleys of sadness
grow
the
gardens of my mind.

Sweet, fragrant
flowers of fantasy
to adorn the bedside
where
my soul lay healing . . .
Broken,
disconsolate and bleeding
from wounds inflicted mercilessly
by
lost love.
But,
worst of all by
SELF.

First Love

I really think that I'm falling in love –
I honestly think that it's true!
I like this feeling it's giving to me.
For me it is something quite new.

My love is quick-witted, attractive, beguiling,
exciting, successful, and smart.
My love's learned to laugh, to cry, and to play:
To think with the head *and* the heart.

To stand on both feet and face life day-to-day,
to be proud of what they've grown to be.
It's a wonderful feeling, this being in love,
for you see, I've learned to love ME!

March

As the legal end of the divorce approaches, old fears come out of hiding I am afraid for myself, for my children, and for life as I would like it to be. The battlefield is set with children as the prize, and heartbreak as the cost. And I find myself as the lone warrior, preparing for a battle whose prize is everything that is important to me.

Dragons

I'm afraid of Invisible Dragons.
They seem to be everywhere.
They have claimed my heart as their fortress,
inhabit my mind as their lair.

I gather my courage to fight them,
but sometimes their force is too strong.
They converge on my mind and my reason.
I fight to hold on – for how long?

I shut the gates to my castle,
and pull the drawbridge up tight.
But the Dragons are never discouraged,
they stalk my soul in the night.

There are no Knights to save me.
I must do it alone.
I hope I can conquer the Dragons
without turning my heart into stone.

What You Break You Pay For

A prized piece fell from the
glass menagerie of life,
fell crashing to the floor and
SHATTERED
into a million pieces.
Dreams of a lifetime lay strewn about,
BROKEN
past repair—
in a heap of
DISARRAY.

The perpetrators came then,
and with spiteful vengeance
stomped on the fragments,
pummelling them into
unrecognizable bits.

Sharp, jagged edges pierced their feet
deeper and deeper with each assault,
but they continued, unheeding,

and, when their feet were sore and bleeding
and they could walk no more,
they bent down, doubled up their fists and
POUNDED
till their hands could
no longer open in LOVE.

When at least they realized what they had done,
they covered their eyes with
blood-soaked hands
and wept.

But no one heard them.

April

With resolution comes relief. The day of the court hearing is Maundy Thursday, it is Spring and Easter season: A time of new life and rebirth. I breathe a sigh of relief, take a deep breath, and step forward on a new path. Through the long days and nights just past I have discovered the value of friends, inner strength, and faith. As I struggle to recover from lost love, I realize the one great love that has helped make all of it bearable.

String Around My Finger

As the trials of life surround me
and often seem too much to bear,
You reach out Your hand to guide me,
to show me how much You care.

When I'm lost and blindly searching
for peace I cannot find,
You touch my heart with Your presence
and calm my troubled mind.

You are my light in the darkness,
my candle in the night:
The strength that keeps me going,
the voice that says I'm all right.

I feel Your arms enfold me
in a warm and tender embrace,
healing my wounded spirit
by the vastness of Your grace.

JULIEANNE GENTZ

This world is full of wonders
I often may not see,
but none is quite so precious
as Your steadfast love for me.

About this Book

Julieanne Gentz found out the hard way that processing the big changes in life alone is not always easy. Follow Julieanne through a year of fear, uncertainty, survival, and discovery while she navigates a divorce as a mother of four. Her honest, soul searching, and insightful poetry speaks to the strength, resilience and love that awaits one at the other end of this highly emotional journey – a journey where lessons learned, and love lost foster a new appreciation for self and provide an inspiration to move forward with confidence, self-compassion, and an openness to life.

About the Author

Julieanne Gentz has been writing her way through the ups and downs of life for as long as she can remember. Beginning as a farm wife with three young children caught in the early stages of the farm crisis of the 80's, she has found herself using the gift of words to work though the challenges life threw at her. She has journaled and written her way through a divorce, second marriage, the adventures of a blended family, and most recently a 13-year journey of love as her husband's Care Partner in his battle with Parkinson's Disease. It is her hope that sharing her struggles and triumphs of moving through life's rough patches and surviving, can help make the journey a little easier for others. Because, after all, that is what life is all about—helping each other.

www.ingramcontent.com/pod-product-compliance
Lightning Source LLC
Chambersburg PA
CBHW022013120526
44592CB00034B/801